Creating A Great First Impression

Being An Effective New Home Sales Center Receptionist

Creating A Great First Impression

Being An Effective New Home Sales Center Receptionist

Steve Hoffacker

AICP, CAASH, CAPS, CGA, CGP, CMP, CSP, MCSP, MIRM

Creating A Great First Impression

Being An Effective New Home Sales Center Receptionist

Cover photo by Steve Hoffacker.

© 2013 by HOFFACKER ASSOCIATES LLC
West Palm Beach, Florida, USA

ISBN: 978-0-615-87422-7

In the new home sales process, new home sales center receptionists can dramatically influence and enhance the overall customer experience and facilitate more sales. When receptionists are used to staff sales, model, or information centers, they perform a vital function that allows the rest of the sales team to be more effective also.

Books, Articles, Blogs & Other Sales Content By Steve Hoffacker

To access or learn about books, eBooks, articles, blogs, commentary, podcasts, videos, webinars, and other content by Steve Hoffacker for anyone who sells products or services for a living, use the sites below.

"Hoffacker Associates" Website
http://stevehoffacker.com

Steve Hoffacker's Amazon.com Author Page
http://amazon.com/author/stevehoffacker

"Steve Hoffacker's Home Sales Insights" Blog
http://homesalesinsights.com

"Steve Hoffacker's Sales Quips" Blog
http://salesquips.com

"Steve Hoffacker's Success Quips" Blog
http://successquips.com

Steve Hoffacker and Hoffacker Associates can be found online at Facebook, Active Rain, Pinterest, Linked-In, Plaxo, Twitter, Goggle+, YouTube, Tumblr, and other business, real estate, and social sites.

Table Of Contents

Preface

As a receptionist in your new home sales center, model home, or information center — or new home pavilion if you represent more than one builder — you have a very special public relations role unlike that of anyone else in your company.

You generally are the first person to interact with the public when they call or visit and want information on your new homes.

I appreciate that you bought this book, or that someone thought enough of you to provide it, and that you are reading it — particularly because of the importance of your role in the new home sales process and the success of your company.

This text has been especially developed for the new home sales center receptionist — or someone else who performs this function of initially greeting people when they enter your new home sales or model center.

You might be a sales assistant (licensed or unlicensed), a host or hostess, or a community representative (licensed or unlicensed) instead of a receptionist — but with essentially the same role.

You are reading this book because you thought enough of yourself to get it and use it — or your builder, developer, sales manager, or sales representative did.

You have indicated by doing this that you want to become an even better sales center or model home receptionist or representative — regardless of how long you have been performing this role.

It shows personal initiative on your part or the willingness to follow the direction of those you are working with to acquire the knowledge to serve your customers, sales team, and company more effectively.

This book was first released as an Amazon Kindle eBook, and now is available as this paperback text.

You can use either one or both to guide your performance. They are essentially the same, with some minor formatting differences.

This distinctive, one-of-a-kind text (I am not aware of any other books or eBooks on this subject) has been written just for you to prepare you for your day-to-day duties as a new home sales center receptionist.

I purposely do not talk about or take into account any specific policies or procedures that your company may desire you to follow. Rather, I discuss your special role in the new home sales process.

This role is not dependent on the size of your organization, the number of homes that your company builds or closes annually, your price point, or your geographic location.

There are certain ways of relating to the public when they contact you or walk into your facility that apply regardless of what you are offering.

Thus, become familiar with the concepts in this text so you can do an outstanding job of representing your company, assisting your sales team, and elevating the overall customer experience of those who visit you.

When people make the decision to visit your sales, model, or information center — or to call for information — you likely will be the first person they encounter.

Therefore, you are responsible for setting the tone and creating the initial atmosphere for their entire sales experience with your company.

You help determine if they will want to do business with your company by the initial impression you create and how they are made to feel. This is a big responsibility and a very important one.

By reading and using the ideas and concepts in this book, you are demonstrating that you are embracing this important function and that you are serious about your role in the new home sales process.

While you won't be taking someone through the entire sales presentation or formalizing a sale yourself with your customers, you can have a big impact on how a customer feels about your homes and your company before they ever talk with a sales associate or representative.

You have the opportunity to help people feel good about working with your sales team and living in one of your homes before they ever get the details about what specifically is available for them to own (except what they may learn from your website).

Of course, the reverse is true.

If people are not made to feel welcome or important when they enter your sales or model center, they are not going to be as inclined to do business with your company.

If they feel that they aren't being taken seriously, your sales team is going to have a much harder time working with them, connecting with them, and making them happy.

People respond well to courtesy, to a friendly greeting, to a bright cheerful atmosphere, and to a feeling that you and your company are glad to see or hear from them when they arrive or call.

This is an important role that you play.

You are the one who initially conveys this to them.

In situations where your office is particularly busy when someone enters, and no one is available to meet with them immediately, your role switches from just making them feel welcome to keeping them from growing weary about the wait.

If they decline to wait for a salesperson and say that they will return at a later time, how much they feel like returning and whether they actually do return will be dependent in large part on how you interact with them as well as their initial impression about your company they get from meeting and speaking with you.

After someone visits your sales or model center, you may still interact with them by telephoning them as requested by your salesperson, by answering their incoming call, or by emailing them a thank you note or information you were asked to send them.

This additional contact will help reinforce their opinion of your company and their desire to do business with you.

An impression once set can either be reinforced or modified — to make it even stronger and more positive than it already is.

You are instrumental in creating this positive, lasting impression of your company — for everyone in your organization.

You might be working for a single builder, or you might be in a central sales pavilion where more than one builder is represented.

Therefore, in some communities or companies, you may have a more active role in taking people to see the models or providing other assistance, but that is not included in this text.

I am interested in helping you be more effective in performing your indispensable duties of greeting and welcoming people to your sales and model center and helping them feel comfortable with your company.

Creating A Great First Impression

Being An Effective New Home Sales Center Receptionist

1

You Are The First Contact

Receptionists Are Special

Over the years, I have seen hundreds and hundreds of new home sales centers and sales offices around the United States.

The offices have been quite varied. Some of them have been located in the garage of the model home — as the normal garage of the home with the overhead door still in place — and some as remodeled space to serve as a sales office and display area.

Some have been free-standing pavilions built just as an information center that would be torn down or removed after the sales operation was completed.

Others have been in trailers or modulars (single-, double-, and triple-wide) located on-site just for the sales program and then removed when they were no longer needed, and some have shared a trailer with construction.

Many have been inside the living space of the model home — in the kitchen, dining room, bedroom, den, or basement.

In golf or tennis communities, sales centers have sometimes been located in the clubhouse.

Still others have been in downtown storefronts, in strip mall shopping centers, as kiosks in shopping centers or hotels, or as suites in office buildings.

Several of these sales centers, model homes, or information centers have had receptionists or sales assistants (by a variety of titles) to initially greet and work with the public, but many have not.

New home sales center receptionists are the one constant — when they are present — among the various shapes, sizes, and designs of the sales or model centers.

Thus, your role as a new home sales center receptionist or sales assistant is quite special.

New home shoppers understand your role as someone who is a non-salesperson and is there to help them and acclimate them to your community.

Sometimes they attempt to take advantage of your position, however, and ask for special treatment or for you to do things for them that your position does not permit— particularly when your sales staff is busy and they don't want to wait their turn.

Just For You

I truly appreciate the very important function that you play and understand how you help the entire sales team as well as your customers.

I created this book especially for you and for the special work that you do in the new home sales process.

You might be a full-time or part-time receptionist, and you might work during the week or on weekends.

You might even have outside employment or attend college in addition to your duties of helping out in the sales center.

Regardless, your role as a receptionist is vitally important to the overall customer experience and the entire success of your company.

You Are The First Contact

Typically you are the first person in your company to speak with or greet customers that come into your sales center or call on the telephone for information — regardless of your official title. This is true even if they are calling for or asking to see someone else.

Whether this is your first day on the job, or you're an experienced veteran, I want you to appreciate how important your role is to the overall success of your company's sales program.

Along with the salespeople and other members of the sales team, you make a significant contribution to the new home sales process.

When customers enter your model center — or telephone for information — you want them to like what they see or hear and experience.

You want them to regard what you are offering well enough to eventually call it "home" and move forward with purchasing a new home from your company.

More than anything else, understand that when people receive a favorable initial impression, such as when they are warmly greeted and welcomed by you, that this helps get the process started successfully.

People have many different reasons for looking for a new home and many different attitudes when they walk through your front door or hold the other end of that phone call (more about this later in Chapters 3 and 4).

Being professional, cordial, pleasant, upbeat, and sympathetic to their needs and questions is an important beginning step to having them liking what you offer and feeling welcome.

Titles Don't Matter

This book focuses on being the very best at greeting and welcoming people to your homes and community.

It doesn't matter how many homes are being built, the price range or style of homes you offer, and whether there is just a single builder or several that you are representing.

It doesn't matter what your office area is called and whether or not it is free standing, attached to a model home, or located among other uses.

To accommodate the many possible names that are used to describe the area where people come for information, I will alternately, as we go along through this text, call your office space a sales center, sales office, model center, showroom, or information center.

Just substitute the correct name for your particular application.

Speaking of names, this book is directed at receptionists who initially greet the public and are responsible for creating a positive initial impression in and around their space.

You might also be called a host, hostess, community representative, or sales assistant with similar responsibilities.

Whatever your formal "business card" title is, I am concerned with your responsibilities and job function and have created this book specifically to help you greet your traffic, establish relationships, and acclimate them to your community.

I know that you are not responsible for making sales so I won't be discussing any sales techniques in this book.

I am concerned with how to represent you and your company in an outstanding way to creating great initial, positive, and lasting impressions.

This is a form of selling, but not the type you typically think of when you hear the word.

First Impressions

Perhaps you have heard it said that you never get a second chance to make a good first impression.

When someone calls your model center on the telephone or walks through your front door, you have a major impact on how that first impression is formed and the quality of it.

What you say, how you say it, the pleasantness in your voice, your tone of voice, the quality and clarity of your voice, how well groomed you are, your attitude, your enthusiasm, your smile (even over the telephone), and how well you maintain the condition of your model center help to establish a quality first impression.

At this initial point of contact, you *are* your company as far as the public is concerned.

They likely have not seen, met, or spoken with anyone else in your organization.

Depending on the nature of their inquiry and their particular needs, they may not ever meet anyone in your company besides you.

You represent everyone in your organization regardless of what position or job function they have. This is true whatever your title is.

Many of your customers will never get past this initial meeting. They may not have an opportunity to meet your builder face-to-face or see many of the other people in your company that work behind the scenes to create a quality product and deliver it to the public. They may never meet a sales representative.

In fact, on their initial visit or contact with your community, some customers may not have an opportunity to speak with anyone other than you or see anything beyond the interior of your sales or model center or any other part of your community that you may show them or allow them to see.

The Customers' Agenda

When you initially talk with customers as they call on the phone or walk through your front door — and even when they email for information — they have many expectations, desires, fears, and misgivings about looking for a new home, visiting a model center, and potentially working with a home builder. I'll talk more about this in Chapter 3 and Chapter 4.

Some of the people you greet or talk with will be demanding and impatient. Others will be quite pleasant and less hurried. Pay attention to these emotions and treat everyone professionally and as cordially as you can.

Since you are the one who greets people when they call or enter your sales center, making them feel at ease and working with them until someone else on your sales team can help them is a big responsibility.

In some cases, you will handle their entire call or visit. Regardless, you must be aware of both what they say as well as what they express non-verbally. It's not always easy to be firm in maintaining control of the conversation and yet pleasant — especially when there are others standing there awaiting your attention also.

The primary thing that people are looking for when they visit or contact your sales center, model home, sales pavilion, or model center is information. You certainly want to help them, but you can only provide so much information or assistance.

Sometimes they have an agenda to complete which may or may not coincide with the way you and your company want to conduct a sales presentation.

They may want a brochure and access to your models as soon as they walk in because they are allowed to get away with that behavior at other sales centers.

Understand that this is a primary need that people have when they visit your sales center, but you have the ability to control the flow of the presentation and let them see the model or receive a brochure on your terms (and those of your company).

Your company may allow you to show the model or direct them to it, but it's to everyone's advantage in your company for your sales representative to convey the brochure. I'll talk more about this strategy later in Chapter 8.

Whatever the policy is of your company regarding what information you are allowed to disseminate and what people must receive from the sales staff, your major role is to welcome people to your model center in a friendly, cordial, and professional way and get their contact information (more on this in Chapter 7).

You may be able to share a little about your opportunity and learn about their basic needs and issues before passing them along to a sales representative to assist them further. However, some people will leave without talking with the salesperson because they weren't allowed to get their own way.

Just remember to maintain your professionalism, even if it may upset or frustrate them initially. You and your company have an agenda also. You have a process that you need to follow.

Showing That You Care

It's one thing to have a slogan posted in your workroom or on your website that you care about the customer or that they come first. It's another to see it in action.

This is why being professional and friendly to everyone — even those who make it very difficult to remember this concept — go a long way in helping people to be receptive to what you and your company have to show them and how you want the presentation to unfold.

People like to be recognized and greeted when they enter your sales center — or to have their incoming phone call answered quickly.

When they tell you why they have contacted you, they really don't want to repeat their story to anyone else.

We all can relate to this based on the number of times we have contacted a customer service department and been passed around and asked the same thing multiple times.

Once you obtain the information on why they have chosen to visit your sales center or what they are looking for in an opportunity — because they volunteer this information or you skillfully obtain it — you can relay what they have said to the sales representative (or other person in your organization) that will be working with them.

This will eliminate the need for anyone else to request this information again, and it will show the customer that you are professional. It's unlikely they will be treated this professionally, courteously, or thoughtfully at other sales centers.

Focus Just On The Greeting

Don't try to do too much. You've plenty of very important work to do.

Even if you are permitted or allowed to get your customers started on looking at the models and providing information about pricing and specific floor plans or locations they might be interested in, this role normally is reserved for the sales representative.

When people enter your sales center, they are looking for information and answers to their questions. They maybe aren't ready to buy anything, but that is not your chief concern.

They may not think that they need to speak to anyone besides you or hear a formal presentation from anyone.

Regardless of what's on their mind or their general attitude when they enter your sales center — or how much they think they are in control of the conversation — you can be a great buffer.

You can greet them, make them feel comfortable, and possibly provide some introductory information — but you won't be engaging them in any type of sales presentation.

Anyway, your customers may have done an in-depth analysis of what you offer on your website.

In fact, they may possess a good understanding of what you offer and may not feel they need much of an orientation but just a few specifics.

Still, the sales representative is really the one to determine their level of interest, their desires, and their buying potential — in addition to answering their specific questions and discussing the opportunities you offer.

Don't apologize for not being able to provide answers to all of their questions. It's this way for a reason.

You get them started by greeting them and possibly offering a brief orientation if there is a short wait for the sales representative to get started. Otherwise, you hand them off and get ready for the next customer — to enter or call.

Making The Handoff

It's important that you realize that people have various reasons for searching for a new home and that many of these reasons for looking for a new home can be accomplished by selecting an existing home ("used" or "resale") as well as a new home — or even a rental home or apartment.

Therefore, an important responsibility of yours as you are working with them is to keep them excited about the fact that they chose to visit you — regardless of their particular motivation.

You don't want a delay in seeing the models or getting the information they seek to upset or discourage them.

Be careful not to mention the word "salesperson" or that they need to meet with one. You are simply going to have them talk with someone more knowledgeable than you about what is available.

Just as the handoff in football must be done correctly to keep from fumbling the ball or interrupting the rhythm of the play, the same is true here. Make the transition smooth and professional.

Briefly explain to the sales representative out loud in front of your customers what they have told you they are looking for and what you have discussed with them so far. Summarize anything else they have told you.

It's not that the sales representative can't read your notes. It's to show your customers that you are professional, that you have been paying attention, and that they are important to you.

It also lets the sales representative hear your customers' names pronounced correctly by you and gets him or her up-to-speed without any lost time or effort.

2

The "Short-List" Challenge

Paying Attention To The "Short-List"

As you are meeting and greeting people who call for information or walk into your sales or model center, you have three main objectives.

In no particular order of importance, you need to record the visit and obtain as much information as possible about who your customers are (including how to contact them), you need to represent your company and your fellow employees well, and you need to do your part to get your company onto each customer's "short list."

In the last chapter I talked about the importance of you representing your company well and how — in addition to being the first contact that your customers have with your company — you might be the only person they meet or speak with during their initial visit or call. I'll talk even more about this in Chapter 5.

As far as the process of making your customers feel welcome and obtaining important information from them, I'll get into the mechanics of the greeting process later in Chapter 7.

So, let's look at your third objective in this chapter — that of getting onto the "short-list" and what this means.

What Is A "Short-List"?

A "short-list" shows the names of those candidates and applicants still in the running for a particular opportunity — a job opening, a project, a purchasing decision, a team, a role, or part in a production.

When someone tries out for a team or a part in a production, the coach or director reviews all of the applicants and watches them perform.

Then a first cut is made. Everyone can't be selected — there are only so many openings so the weaker ones are trimmed from further consideration.

Based on their tryouts or auditions, some people just didn't do as well or weren't as strong as people they were going up against for that particular opportunity.

Those still in the running will have made the first so-called "short-list" — although it may not be all that short at this point.

Then, there will be a second round of cuts — and possibly more depending on how many people still remain and the number of positions or opportunities open.

The same holds true when you apply for a position at a new community that is opening or when you want to relocate.

You submit an application or resume, it gets reviewed, and you make it through the initial screening or you don't.

You may get an interview which shows that you made it through the first screening.

You might make it to the final cut of just a few applicants ("short-list").

The true short-list contains the actual finalists — typically just a few more names than will eventually be selected.

If someone's name is not on this list, there will be no chance of making the team or getting the position this time.

Using A "Short-List" Is Quite Common

Using a short-list is more common than we might think. In fact, many of us use quire regularly.

When you interview someone for a job as a babysitter, housekeeper, assistant, landscaper, accountant, auto mechanic, computer repair, or other position for your home or business, you likely will go through a similar selection and review process.

Sometimes, the short-list process can be informal such selecting a place to eat lunch or dinner. You start with a list of places or cuisines that you think you are in the mood for and narrow down the choices until you select just one.

Everyone has done this a little more formally when it comes time to select a major appliance (refrigerator, range, washer, or dryer), a new car or truck, a TV, a computer, or an RV.

You start by doing your research and identifying the brand, model, and features you want. Then you identify various dealers or stores that offer it.

As you progress toward your final decision, you cull the list and refine it until it has just a couple of names remaining (including the one you are going to choose) — then eventually just one.

When customers visit your office looking for a new home, they have other builders and other opportunities from which to select — including resales.

You have to impress them enough with what you offer and the type of company you are to make it onto their short-list — and continue to stay there — if you ever plan on them purchasing their new home with you and your company.

This is a significant challenge and one that you are in a great position to help facilitate.

Your Role In The Process

Understanding that people have a short-list and use it — whether it's actually written down or just kept in their heads — to make important decisions, your role as a receptionist is to consciously and intentionally work to get your company onto that list with each person that you meet as they visit your sales center or those you talk with on the phone or by email.

It's not up to you to make a presentation, and some people may not like or want the opportunities available or feel that their needs can be addressed by what you offer as a builder. That is not your direct concern.

However, you need to focus on making sure that when you hand them off to a sales representative or they hang up the phone or walk out the door, you have done everything in your power to establish a great impression so that they will want to keep you and your company on their short-list.

They won't be purchasing directly from you, but the impression you create can help them feel very good about doing business with you and your company — provided that you offer a home that appeals to them and meets their needs.

Your demeanor, the way you interact with them, and the way you make them feel welcome is so important in creating that great initial impression — even if they determine that they don't want to live in your homes or community because of their particular needs.

There still is a positive word-of-mouth referral potential there.

As long as you are confident that you have done your part to get or keep your company onto their short-list — even if they eventually choose a home elsewhere — you will have succeeded.

The Dynamics Of A Short-List

We tend to think that we have to do something to make it onto someone's short-list when often we just need to focus on remaining there.

Frequently, people will come into your model or information center with a predetermined list of builders, homes, and locations that they want to look at, consider, and evaluate — both new and existing, unless they have already ruled out purchasing an existing (resale) home.

Therefore, your company very likely is already on their list or they wouldn't be visiting or considering you. So, the key is staying there.

People are looking for ways to eliminate you from their lists and arrive at their final choice by seeing who is left on their lists when they are done.

When someone shops the marketplace, they are going through a selection process that involves crossing off the opportunities that don't work for them. They are paring their short-list until it gets down to one or two serious contenders.

If you already are on someone's short-list — consciously or not — when they visit or contact you, your very important focus and function is to help insure — to the extent that you can — that you stay on their list.

You can't control what happens once they begin working with the sales representative to look at or evaluate specific floor plans that might meet their needs or expectations, specific locations available for them, and pricing plans — and how well they feel that they like what is being presented.

Nevertheless, while you are working with someone and orienting them to your opportunities, you can help them feel good about their visit to your company.

Do all that you can to create a good, solid initial impression and then to reinforce it during your contact with them.

3

Major Short-List Considerations

Appealing To People's Needs

As people are evaluating what you have to offer, they are comparing it to other opportunities in the marketplace.

They also are assessing how well what you offer fits with what they are looking for in a new home and the reasons they are considering making a move.

There are many factors that motivate people to look for a new home, and as you hear them mentioned in conversation you will want to note them and key in on them.

You'll want to make sure your notes are passed along to the salesperson who will talking with them about your homes.

Emphasize and underscore the strength of your location, your company, your amenities, and other features you offer when your customers mention that these are what they are seeking.

Depending on what's specifically important to them, your customers are looking at and evaluating such factors as the quality of the investment that your homes and community offer, the convenience of your location, the natural beauty of it, the status or prestige your homes or location offer, the lifestyle opportunities available, the costs of living, the designs and layouts available, and features provided.

What you offer is being contrasted with other opportunities your customers are aware of in the market. — including other builders, resales, rentals, and even remaining where they are currently living.

So keep these variables and factors in mind — especially as it pertains to staying on someone's short-list — as you are greeting, meeting, and talking with your customers.

Finding a floor plan that someone wants to own and live in is only part of the challenge for new home shoppers. There are many other factors that they need to consider in their selection process, and these will have an impact on which builders or homes make it onto or remain on their short-list.

Financial

One of the reasons that someone looks for a new or different home is financial.

They might be looking for a higher quality investment than what their current home or location offers them.

Maybe they are seeking a greater opportunity for appreciation in a newer or more prestigious neighborhood. Possibly they owned a home previously and have sold it and now want to reinvest that money in a new (or different) home.

Some people have never owned a home before. They are tired of renting and now would like to own a home to begin building some equity and taking advantage of the interest deductions and other tax breaks that are afforded homeowners.

Still others have the financial ability to desire, invest in, and support a second or third residence — to actually live in occasionally as a vacation or seasonal home or rent out for investment income.

An additional financial aspect concerns the maintenance and upkeep of their home.

Many people — whether they are experienced homeowners or looking for their first home — have decided that getting a new home is likely to require less out-of-pocket expenses for maintenance items than remaining in their current home or choosing an existing home.

Additionally, the manufacturers of many of the components and systems used in the construction of a new home warranty such items as appliances, materials, and fixtures for specific periods of time.

One other financial concern is the commitment to the homeowners association and the services and facilities it provides.

Many people select their new home both for what is available to enhance their lifestyle experience and how it impacts their monthly housing budget.

Location, Location, Location

Another reason why people seek a new home (or a different home than they have now even if it isn't brand new) is for a change of location (or scenery).

I'm sure you've heard that it's location, location, location when it comes to real estate.

People desire a location or neighborhood that is more convenient for them to travel to work, school, children's activities, friends, or relatives. Sometimes it's just because it's a prettier area or closer to shopping or recreational activities that they enjoy.

Maybe moving from where they are now to be closer to freeway interchanges, commuter train stations, or the airport is important to them.

Some people are seeking a vacation or seasonal residence, and they are choosing a location because it is close to friends or family or because of the climate or recreational opportunities available.

Some are relocating for job-related reasons and they are looking for a location in their new city that seems convenient to their new office.

Depending on the location or neighborhood that might be selected, either a new home or an existing home could suffice so keep this in mind. Established neighborhoods of older homes in prestigious parts of town have their charm and reputation.

Even in brand new, amenitized communities, a home built within the past couple of years might be available — offering the same location and recreational benefits as a new one in that community.

Some may desire a location that they believe represents better value or quality or one that they think has a more desirable address or better chance of appreciation than their existing neighborhood, and some people may desire to be in a different school district or taxing district.

Location is important, and people have many variables as far as location is concerned to factor into their decisions on a new home.

Status

In addition to looking for a change in location for financial or convenience reasons, another reason for desiring a new (or different) home is for prestige or status.

People may want a new (or different) home that is larger, more expensive, more unusual, more elaborate, or more up-to-date than the one they have been living in — and more than that of their friends, relatives, or colleagues.

Possibly they are looking for a home that's on the water, on the golf course, on a preserve, in a wooded setting, on a hillside, set off by itself, at the end of a cul-de-sac. or one that makes a statement.

Perhaps it is one that boasts an unusual floor plan, building materials, or exterior design. Maybe they want all of the latest technology and state-of-the-art features.

Remember that finding a very attractive home in an established neighborhood can satisfy this requirement.

It's not always a new home in a new community that is desired for a prestigious location or design so this challenge needs to be taken seriously.

Lifestyle

Another reason for desiring a new home (or a different one) is a change of lifestyle, especially moving to a community or neighborhood that offers recreational opportunities.

There might be limited or no particular recreational amenities where people currently live, and they are looking forward to finding a community that offers activities such as tennis, swimming, golf, or dining.

Maybe they are looking for trails, sidewalks, or street lights where they and their children can walk, skate, jog, or ride their bikes in relative safety and not have to worry about traffic.

Security is a big issue for many people today.

They are looking for a gated community or one with roving patrols or limited access. They might be looking for a location that they deem to be safer than their current neighborhood for greater peace-of-mind.

Of course, families with children (or visiting grandchildren) are always looking for greater opportunities for their children to grow up in a safe, healthy atmosphere or to have structured activities available for them.

People also like looking at and living in attractive communities (new home communities or existing neighborhoods) with beautiful landscaping and ones in which community regulations maintain the appearance of their community and the quality of their investment.

In addition to the social and recreational activities that frequently define lifestyle, ease of maintenance is another.

Many people are looking for a community where much or all of the exterior of their home is cared for (including landscaping, lawn cutting and sometimes painting).

Regardless, a new home has far less maintenance than an existing home because the appliances, fixtures, finishes, and other components are new and much of it is warrantied.

Space

Still another reason for desiring a new home (or a different one) is either more or less space in the home itself — and possibly the yard around the home. As family sizes change, people find that they need or desire either a larger home or a smaller one — or possibly one configured differently, with more or less space in specific rooms or areas of their home.

Families that are growing (or ones where adult children or elderly parents have moved in) need a larger home with four or more bedrooms. They need family rooms, bonus rooms, often three-car garages, and possibly a large yard for a pool and a place for the kids to play.

Conversely, families which have raised their children and have seen their children start households of their own, or move on to college or the military, require or desire less space to manage — they may want two bedrooms with a den or three bedrooms.

They still want storage space and space for guests and for the children (and grandchildren) to come home and visit, but they foresee maintaining less space than they have currently.

Also, many people today, regardless of family size or how many bedrooms they require, want space for a home office or media center. Some people desire a fitness or workout area as well.

New household formation (divorce, marriage, leaving home as an adult, graduation from college, or completion of military service) is another factor in causing people to seek a new or different residence.

For some this also will be their first home — with space or layout considerations being less of a concern than just finding a comfortable home within their budget in a location they like.

"New"

In looking for a home, many people seek a new home — and not just a different home or a newer one than what they might have currently — because they want something totally *new*.

Many reasons for seeking or desiring a different home can be satisfied by either a new home or an existing one — or even a rental. Sometimes though, only a new home will suffice.

While some relatively new homes can provide many advantages and are similar to brand new homes in many respects, usually only a new home can provide the latest, most up-to-date technology or state-of-the-art features.

Only a new home can satisfy those people who want to know that they have chosen the cabinets, colors, features, type of flooring, and other personalized features that they want.

They know that only a new home can give them the peace-of-mind and comfort level of knowing that no one else has ever occupied their home previously.

Only a new home comes with that unmistakable new home "smell" and "feel."

For people that want something brand new, only a new home will do.

The Short-List Summary

For financial, location, status, lifestyle, and space reasons or motivation — plus the prospect of having a "new" home — people are investigating whether anything they see in the marketplace can do a better job of appealing to them and satisfying their concerns than the home they have now.

They are looking at new homes, nearly new homes, and older homes. They might be considering rentals as well.

Notice also that many of the concerns or considerations that people have overlap — that location or financial concerns can be measured in lifestyle or status ways.

As their search takes them to various types and locations of homes, the one concern they have that can't be met anywhere else besides something like you and your company are offering is a brand new home.

While some established neighborhoods with beautiful landscaping and a prestigious address have their appeal, and while a nearly new home in a neighborhood such as yours can afford many of the same attributes as a brand new home, there is no getting around a brand new home for the choices, selections, design, and newness it offers.

So as you are conscious of people interviewing and evaluating your company and location as far as its suitability for them and their needs, keep in mind that your objective is to make it onto or to remain on their short-list.

Listen to what they are saying and make sure to portray your community and your homes in a good light with respect to their general concerns — to the extent that they share or verbalize their concerns and that you are allowed or permitted to discuss what you offer before they meet with your sales representative.

4

Additional Short-List Concerns

Factors Affecting A Decision

As exciting or challenging as it is for people to be looking at and considering a new home for the reasons just mentioned, it also can be overwhelming and intimidating.

Therefore, be prepared for people to display a range of emotions when they visit your sales center.

People may be confused about what they really want, and your role in helping them feel at ease in a stressful situation is quite important.

In fact, people who are seeking a new home may have just as many or even more inherent fears and apprehensions about the process of choosing a new home that mitigate or offset their excitement.

This is why your role in initially greeting them and welcoming them in a cordial and professional way is so significant.

Money Issues

Money is a major issue when people are looking for a new home.

Either consciously or subconsciously, they are mindful of the financial obligation.

I mentioned the financial reasons or implications why someone might be interested in finding a new home — higher quality investment, better chance of appreciation, less maintenance expense, more efficient, more prestige, and similar reasons.

There are just as many concerns that people have of a financial nature that hold them back from making a decision. Be aware of them and do your best to keep people more focused on why they want a new home rather than on any apprehensions they might have.

Buying a home represents the largest single investment for most people, and regardless of whether people have a fifteen or a thirty year mortgage and what the actual terms are of their loan, this is a very long time for most people to make a commitment.

They might wonder if it is wise to make such a serious commitment, or what would happen if they lose their source of income.

Even when people are paying cash, they want to make sure that they are making a wise investment with their money.

The financial aspects of selecting a new home (or even an existing home) are significant — possibly even monumental.

This is challenging and stressful for many people.

There are so many parts to the financing picture, such as interest rates, loan type, terms, amount to be financed, the initial deposit, closing costs, lenders, application and origination fees, credit checks, loan committees, verification of income and funds to close, appraisals, inspections, and title companies.

It can be quite intimidating for a potential buyer.

Working With A Builder

Another area of concern for consumers is doing business with a builder.

People may have heard or read stories of how a builder has gone out of business, not finished what he or she started, been difficult to work with, or converted deposits.

They need to be reassured that your company is a reputable organization.

While you may not have a direct role in explaining the strength of your company to consumers, people require the assurance that your company can deliver a quality new home and that it will be worth the investment.

Being greeted by someone like you when they enter your sales center is a great start for having people feel good about the possibility of doing business with your company.

You help to create an atmosphere of trustworthiness.

The Idea Of Change

Another real concern that people have is fear of the unknown (or fear of making changes).

While the concept of choosing and moving into a new home is exciting and may be what people really need to do, it presents many unknowns that may scare or concern them. They are often fearful or uneasy of changing the *status quo*.

People already know the most convenient routes to work, school, friends, relatives, shopping and leisure time activities. They already know their neighborhood.

They already know their current home — even with its shortcomings.

A move will mean adjustments and possibly finding new friends and locating new services and stores or routes to work and other activities.

Moving Itself

Speaking of moving, people are concerned about the physical and emotional process of making the move itself. Changing their place of residence is disruptive.

Occasionally items can get lost or broken when everything that someone owns is wrapped or boxed up and loaded onto a truck.

Then, there is the living out of those boxes when it takes weeks or months to get every box unpacked and items put where they will live in the new home.

Unfortunately, this is part of the moving process, but careful planning should help to keep such interruptions and inconveniences to a minimum.

You need to be a cheerleader here.

Your role is to help reassure people of the positive side of moving into a new home and the opportunities it offers.

The Decision

Of course, some people will fear or worry over making the actual commitment or the decision, regardless of what they decide to do.

This will happen whether they are buying a new home or resale — or even staying when they are due to indecision or finding that this is the easiest choice for them to make.

Some people reach decisions very quickly, while others require dozens of facts and take a long time to make a decision.

Many even second-guess themselves or try to change their minds after they have made a decision, and some people will check with friends or relatives and actually hope to be talked out of a decision.

Still others will visit your new home community looking for reasons why they shouldn't buy from you.

Be careful of providing your opinion — even when specifically asked for it — about the wisdom of them finding a new home and moving into it.

Keep them focused on the positives of looking at a new home and leave your personal views or advice out of the discussion.

It's human nature to want to often friendly advice — especially when asked for it or they seem to want it.

Nevertheless, this can really be counterproductive to your overall sales effort.

Maintaining Focus

So, as exciting and interesting as it might be for someone to think about acquiring and moving into a new home, there are all these issues or concerns that people may have about actually doing something.

Some of these issues or concerns are stronger than others, but they need to be overcome or set aside by your sales team before the sale can happen.

Because of the emotional conflict and stress that some people face over making a decision — even though they act like they want to make a move — they may decide to forego a decision on acquiring a new home altogether and just remain in their current home.

Sometimes by comparison, remaining in their present home seems more attractive, and certainly easier and less stressful for them.

They just are unable or unwilling to cope with the process of selecting and moving into a new home.

You are the one who must create a very strong, positive initial impression of your company and your community or neighborhood.

This will affect the sales presentation that they are about to receive as well as their attitude about your entire company.

Obviously, you cannot be responsible for the content or quality of the sales presentation that they will receive from the sales representative who is authorized to give that presentation.

Nevertheless, you can make sure that as long as customers are in your control, that they will receive friendly, courteous, and professional service.

5

It's Your Arena

Starting Off Strong

Unless you have a security station for people to stop at and pass through on the way to your information or model center, you are the first contact that each customer will have with your community or company.

You are responsible for setting the initial tone and for creating the proper lasting impression of your company, community, or homes — before they ever meet with anyone else or see much of what you have to offer.

The physical presentation of what your customers see, hear, smell, and experience when they approach, arrive at, enter, and remain in your information center area must create a strong initial impression:

Make sure that the areas people might see or experience are clean and fresh.

Look for signs of ants, spiders, bees, wasps, and other pests — clean up any traces of them that you see. Also, look for noticeable fingerprints, dust, and stains — and remove them.

Be aware of food smells, clutter, messiness, or other distractions — regardless of what area in your sales center they might be or who may have generated them.

You Own Your Space

When people enter your sales office, sales center, model home, model center, or information center — however the space is configured or appointed — they are stepping into your arena. When they call you on the phone, they are contacting your arena.

You don't just manage the physical space, the way information is conveyed to them, and the way they feel while they are working with you. You own it. You are totally responsible for what go on there.

Whatever the space looks like, smells like, or feels like to your customers (and even their friends or relatives who might accompany them) is directly under your control.

While you are not responsible for the decorating, you are responsible for what people experience when they enter and remain in your space — the neatness, appearance, and feeling it conveys.

The brightness, cheeriness, lack of clutter, cleanliness, and sense of order are what you control. If anything doesn't measure up to what you want or expect — and by extension, what your customers should expect — change it.

This is, after all, your place of business.

Your responsibility is to greet people when they enter, welcome them to your company and your new home offerings, and help them feel good about their initial impression.

Therefore, anything that detracts from your ability to do this is something you cannot accept — and neither can the rest of your team.

You Have A Sales Function

As much as anyone else in your company, you have a sales function. Don't worry about your official title, you are selling initial impressions, your company, and attitudes.

You won't be conducting sales presentations and attempting to get a deposit check from anyone, but you make it more likely to happen by creating a great first impression where people feel welcome and comfortable.

People must be positively impressed about what you offer as soon as they enter your model or information center and meet you. Otherwise the likelihood of them eventually purchasing a home from your company is greatly diminished.

In fact, the rest of your team is counting on you to make that initial sale so that your customers will be ready to live in one of your homes — assuming that your company builds a home they like that is within their budget.

At no point should you ever feel or verbalize that it's not your job to do something that will enhance the overall experience of your customers. This includes mopping up a spill, vacuuming the floor, dusting the furniture and displays, serving refreshments, stocking the restrooms, emptying a trashcan, and anything else that requires attention in order to maintain a showroom appearance and experience.

Your sales representative, your builder, or others in your company that actually work with your customers to help them select a new home may never get their opportunity without you making the initial sale that convinces your customers that they are welcome and that you care.

Impressions Really Count

It's often the little things that affect people in such significant ways. Sometimes they won't even realize that they are forming positive or negative opinions — only that something feels comfortable or that it doesn't.

It's things they experience on their way to learn about what you offer that need to convey a quality impression — signage, parking lot area, sidewalks, roadways, landscaping, and displays.

It's what they experience before they open the door to your model center. It's what they remember from being with you. It's the collective time they spend with the sales representative. It's all of that.

It's also what they see and remember as they walk out your door and get in their car to leave after a presentation. A sloppy parking lot, unpleasant smells, or other types of disorder can undermine an otherwise well done presentation.

Remember the saying about actions speaking louder than words? Pay particular attention to the messages that your physical environment is conveying to your customers.

Anything that detracts from a strong initial impression that your customers receive, or that they form, when they arrive and remain in your community or model home — or what they take away with them — needs to be noted by you and reported to the person responsible for rectifying those issues.

If it's within your power to take care of any situation you encounter, then you should just do it — without giving it a second thought.

Beginning Outside

In terms of the general setting when someone enters your sales or information center, you need to make sure that your showroom area and any other places that you intend to show to your customers or allow them to go are presentable.

You want to create a very strong initial impression that makes people like and respect what they will see and hear from you and the other team members.

Start outside and work your way into your interior space. Begin at the parking area. Review the entire impression that the parking area gives — the general condition, the cleanliness of the surface (with no major puddles after a rain or any accumulation or sand, gravel, dirt, or leaves), the parking stops in good condition and anchored where they are supposed to be, and the landscaping around the parking lot being neat and well groomed.

Make sure there are no tripping hazards anyplace.

The parking lot is one of the first things people see when they approach your model center and the first thing that you are directly responsible for inspecting. It's also one of the last things the see and remember as they are leaving.

If it's just a matter of picking up a branch that has fallen or picking up some litter that has been carelessly left behind or blown there by the wind, you have the ability to do that and should.

Approach & Entry

Look at the sidewalk and entry to your model home, sales center, or information center. It should be clean with no debris, dirt, snow, leaves, sand, gravel, mulch chips, or puddles on the walking surface or so close to the walkway and entrance that it creates a visual distraction or unsure footing. Pay attention to anything that might trip your guests.

Remember the look you are going for is "showroom condition." Think of this as a movie set where everything is in place exactly as it should be and in perfect condition so that nothing will spoil the shot.

Pay particular attention to the exterior entry mat and the entry door. Clean both as necessary throughout the day.

Have a couple of spare mats that can be replaced on rainy or wet days when the mat becomes very wet or soiled. It may need to be changed out more than once in a given day.

If your mats are so large and heavy that you need help in moving them, then arrange for someone to be available to help you do this.

Nothing spoils a million dollar look as quickly as a muddy or soiled entrance mat where it looks like no one cares about the appearance — or where the mud is tracked into the sales center.

Pick up liter as necessary and really monitor what people see as they approach your front door.

Remember that people are looking for reasons to keep you on their list or remove you, so make sure this initial impression — before they ever open your front door and engage you — is strong, positive, and lasting.

Reception Area

Make sure that the space around your reception desk is inviting and unencumbered to allow room for your customers to enter and speak with you without them feeling like they are being "huddled" at the door.

If necessary, have your reception desk repositioned far enough away from the entrance door to accomplish this.

Keep the top of your reception desk or counter free of all materials except a phone, computer, notepad, and one or more blank customer information cards.

Do not store any papers, folders, or materials (including incoming or outgoing mail or written messages) in view of the public. You don't want them to see, pick up, or take them because these don't pertain to them. The public should not see anything that is not specifically intended for them.

Many offices leave flyers, business cards, and other literature sitting out for people to take so the public is accustomed to picking up or handling things that are within their view or grasp.

Make sure that the volume of any background music (radio or CDs) is comfortable for an office setting and that it is tuned to an "easy listening" format. The music should not compete with conversation or be distracting.

Of course, there is no smoking allowed by anyone in your model center — or anyplace near an entrance where the smoke could blow back inside.

After each customer leaves your area (unless someone else immediately enters and occupies your attention), check to see that the furniture is positioned properly and that there are no beverage containers or other materials remaining from the previous customers.

All magazines, newspapers and other literature that you intend to have out should be *current* and neatly arranged.

The floors should be free of all debris, water, dirt, food particles (if you serve cookies), mud or other stains or hazards — regardless of how they got there.

Have a mop, electric broom, "Swifter," upright vacuum, handheld vacuum, carpet sweeper, and/or other cleaning supplies ready to correct the appearance of the tiled and carpeted floor areas.

Pick up any noticeable debris from the carpet such as leaves or scraps of paper and use the carpet sweeper or handheld vacuum as necessary.

Display Area

You may not use the display area very much or at all with your customers, but it is important for you to monitor its condition and keep it presentable throughout the day.

Visually, your customers will see it soon after they enter your office. They may wander off to it while they are waiting on you or the sales representative to engage them.

You may have occasion to use the displays to begin acquainting them with who you are as a company and what opportunities you offer — depending on how your specific role and duties are defined.

Keep the display area just as neat and clean as you do your general reception area. Pay particular attention to the displays themselves since they will show fingerprints and other marks very easily.

Have glass cleaner, all-purpose cleaner, furniture polish, dusting cloths, and other supplies ready to maintain the appearance of displays, furniture, mirrors, molding, windows, and other areas where fingerprints are likely to show.

If you are charged with keeping your scale model or site plan current and up-to-date, make sure that is done as soon as you get the information.

Make sure all lamps and lights are turned on and fully lit. Replace any bulbs you can reach (with a supply that you keep on hand), and know who to call to replace bulbs inaccessible or too high for you to reach.

Do not tolerate burned out light bulbs for more than overnight. If you or one of the other members of your team can't replace them immediately, they should be replaced by maintenance or construction no later than the start of the next business day.

Behind The Scenes

Your customers will take in more than you sometimes intend, so spare no effort in making your *entire* model center neat, presentable, and fresh.

There should be no burned out light bulbs anywhere — not just in the reception or display areas — and no dirty floors or floor coverings anywhere. You never know what your customers might see.

Inspect all public areas (restrooms, kitchen, and individual offices) and make certain that trash containers are emptied frequently, paper products and soap are well supplied, and that they are ready for customers to see and use them.

All desks and table tops should be free of unnecessary materials — even if customers won't be using them but merely seeing them as they walk about your model center, showroom, or sales office.

Make sure that anything that might be cooked or heated up in your kitchen — even if it is for customers — does not leave a lingering smell or odor unless it's chocolate chip cookies or something pleasant like that.

Popcorn smells great when it's first cooked but becomes more unpleasant as time passes. Even coffee loses its pleasant aroma when it gets stale.

Lasagna (especially when the cheese burns), Chinese food, and anything with garlic or other pungent spices are foods to keep out of the sales center.

Sales Vehicles

If your customers are driven to models or available homes away from your main model center, and company vans or golf carts are used, these are an extension of the information center and fall under your purview.

The vehicles must be clean and presentable at all times.

Inspect them at the start of the day and as frequently as possible throughout the day. This does not apply to the personal cars of the sales representatives — just the company vehicles.

They also need to be filled with gas or charged (electric vehicles or carts) on a regular basis.

Be prepared to vacuum, mop, clean the window glass (this is huge and will spoil an otherwise pleasant experience for your customers), and pick up any litter left in the van, car, or golf cart — regardless of how it got there.

Make arrangements to have someone on your team wash the exteriors on a regular basis (daily if necessary) — whether it is done on-site or taken to a commercial car wash.

Instruct all drivers to keep the radio turned off when they exit the vehicles so that it will be in the off position the next time it used with customers.

Do not allow smoking inside the vehicles by staff or customers — as a courtesy to others and to help keep the vehicles as fresh and clean as possible.

Once smoking occurs in a vehicle, it lingers for a very long time and is quite noticeable to non-smokers.

The vehicles need to be serviced on a regular basis so plan a maintenance program with your manager that can help insure that "downtime" is kept to a minimum.

Make arrangements with the dealer from which you obtained the vehicles to provide "loaners" similar to what you are using when your vehicles need to be serviced.

Model Home

If the model home is part of your sales or model center because you are physically located in a bedroom, the garage, the kitchen, the den, or otherwise attached or joined to it, then you need to be responsible for the appearance of that home (inside and out) which essentially is an extension of your space.

Several times throughout the day, walk through the model and inspect it — while making sure that you can see or hear if someone new enters your reception area.

You are looking for dirt, smudges, fingerprints, missing accessories, broken items, stains, or anything else that takes away from the showroom condition that it was in when you unlocked the model (and by extension, your sales center) in the morning.

Address and correct the items that you can. Report the others for prompt action and attention.

Remember, this is your space and you are responsible for the way it looks and appears to your customers. Do not settle for anything less that the best possible condition.

If there are other models also or the model is detached from where you are located, you need to have oversight of it or them.

This means you need to be aware of what is going on and check them as you can but not as frequently as the attached model because this could take you away from your post (and your ability to greet new customers) for extended periods of time.

Get your sales representatives to report to you items that they see during their presentations or while they are doing periodic inspection tours throughout the day.

Don't Overlook The Small Stuff

More than any one thing that determines how well customers like your homes and your company — and ultimately whether they will purchase one of your homes — is how they feel when they arrive, the general impressions they form while they are with you, and the lasting impression that stays with them when they leave.

You have a large contribution to make in that respect because you engage them first, you control the environment where they initially experience your company, and you monitor the sales environment to make sure that the strongest impressions possible are conveyed through what people see, smell, and experience.

Don't discount even the smallest details. Remember the short-list.

Nothing is unimportant if it affects how someone might feel about how welcome or comfortable they are in your space, what they think about the quality of your company, or how they might imagine themselves living in one of your homes.

You never know when someone might take away as part of their overall impression and experience the feeling that something was uncomfortable or unappealing — that had nothing to do with the new home opportunities available for them.

Don't give them that chance.

You have that power to make sure they have a great experience.

6

Greeting
The Public

At The Ready

Regardless of what type of community or product you are representing, the style or configuration of your sales center, and what time of the day it is — whether you're waiting for your first customer of the day or a dozen people already have visited — you should always be anticipating and expecting a customer to telephone or walk through the door at any moment.

Your attitude and demeanor should convey this also. It should look like you are expecting them. That's why you're open, and that's why you're there.

You've already made sure that anyone who visits or contacts you will have a great experience because you are dedicated to creating the climate for that strong positive initial impression and pleasant feeling to occur.

When someone contacts you, it should seem as though you have been waiting just for their call or visit and that you have nothing else as important as greeting them and making them glad they decided to call or visit your sales center.

Don't appear or sound overly eager — as if they are your only chance at making a sale.

Just show them the professional courtesy and appreciation that demonstrates they are welcome and that you truly are interested in helping them.

Because you should be expecting a customer to walk through the door or telephone you at any moment, your sales center should reflect this attitude.

It must be in showroom condition at all times. Nothing should be out of place.

Don't be caught by surprise.

This is your responsibility — take ownership of how your sales environment looks. It literally reflects on your ability to manage the appearance of your sales center and to create the professional experience that you want for your customers.

A Friendly Beginning

I've already mentioned some of the apprehensions and concerns that people have when they visit a new home sales center (Chapter 4).

I've also stressed the importance of making it onto your customer's short-list (Chapter 2). This is your key objective.

Being professional when you greet people, demonstrating a willingness to help them, and helping them acclimate to your community will get the relationship started well.

People may be tired, frustrated, or weary from the process of looking at new homes, talking with salespeople, evaluating their choices, and devoting time and energy to their search.

An understanding and pleasant response from you will go a very long way toward creating a great impression and making friends.

As you greet the people walking into your information center, you probably are seated behind a reception desk or counter. You should stand up as they enter.

This is a sign of respect to your visitors and a friendly gesture as well.

You do not have to get out from behind your desk or counter and walk toward the customers, although it's fine if you do.

Primarily just stand and wait for them to approach you. Again, don't appear too eager, just friendly.

By standing, it also puts you at eye-level with your customers. If you remain seated, they likely will be looking down to talk to you.

When you are momentarily busy concluding an incoming telephone call or working with another customer when someone enters, immediately acknowledge their presence and indicate that you see them — use direct eye contact, a gracious smile, and a polite gesture.

The Importance Of "Welcome"

As soon as your customers are physically close enough to you for you to begin a conversation, give them a sincere, warm smile and begin this way: *"Hi, welcome to ..."* (adding the name of your community or the name of your builder — or both).

This is such a simple yet powerful greeting, and one that is rarely used in new home sales centers.

Let your customers know you appreciate them.

The word "welcome" when used sincerely is a very powerful and comforting word.

Don't ever compromise your professional greeting by saying something like, *"Hi, can I help you?"* or *"Are you here to see the models?"*

In just the single word "welcome," you are conveying messages such as: *"We're glad to see you," "We've been expecting you," "We think you'll enjoy your time with us," "We want you to feel at-ease here," "We've created this model home experience to share with you,"* and *"Relax and enjoy yourself."*

Leave no doubt that you are happy to see them, that they are welcome, and that they are important.

Even if you have to maintain conversations with two or more sets of customers who are in your area at the same time, toggle between them and keep them engaged.

Fielding An Incoming Call

If it's an incoming phone call that is the initial contact rather than the physical walk-in visit, you should answer the phone with the same warm greeting that you would use if you were meeting them in person. Your smile should be noticeable by the people calling you, and you should answer by the second ring.

Don't be concerned that answering the call immediately may appear a little aggressive or overly-eager because three or more rings before answering can show a lack of readiness.

There's also a chance the caller could hang up — thinking no one was going to answer or that they would get a voice message.

Sometimes there are delays in the way phones connect and what sounds like two or three rings on the caller's end may only be one ring on your phone.

Thus, answering the phone as soon as you hear it is the best policy. You never know when the caller is about to hang up because they think no one is answering.

Since they aren't actually present, you can't welcome them to your community in those terms. However, you certainly can thank them for calling and make it sound like you have been waiting to help them.

Also, avoid putting them on hold for any period of time.

If you need to delay talking with them while you attend to someone in front of you or you need to transfer them to someone else, check back every 15-20 seconds to let them know that you remember they are holding and that their call is still important to you.

Getting a number where you can call them back may be the best policy. Plus it allows you to obtain and note their phone number along with their name.

Your job is to help provide information or hand them off to someone else who can help them.

You don't need to close the caller on an appointment to visit, but if they indicate they want to visit at a certain time go ahead and note it.

You may need to close them on a time for you to call back with an answer to their question or to set an appointment then for them to visit.

Introducing Yourself

Your major role as a receptionist is to greet and welcome customers to your model center or new home community — in-person as they visit or by phone when they call.

You want to help them feel comfortable as you begin breaking down some of the fears and apprehensions (as I presented in Chapter 4) they have about entering a new home model or sales center and working with a salesperson.

While you aren't a salesperson, the process of helping them to feel at ease starts with you.

After you greet them with a smile and your welcoming message, introduce yourself — on the phone as well as in-person. Just your first name is sufficient.

This is an additional part of the welcoming process which helps to establish a friendly tone.

Do this even if you are wearing a name tag. Some people feel that the name tag suffices. It is only a reference.

Introduce yourself so they feel comfortable addressing you by name. Also, your name may be pronounced somewhat differently than it looks on you name badge so let your customers hear the correct way to say your name — from you. Even repeat it if necessary.

When you take the first step and introduce yourself, it also lets the customers know whom they're talking to and may cause them to reflexively give their names as well. This, in turn, facilitates completion of the customer information card or computer record.

Many receptionists feel awkward about shaking hands with customers, but this is another part of the welcoming process that helps to set a friendly tone.

If you feel comfortable shaking hands with your customers, and it seems appropriate, good ahead and do this.

People enjoy working with someone who seems genuinely happy and excited about what they are doing.

What better way for someone to feel enthusiastic about working with your company than to be met and greeted by someone like you who is displaying a big, enthusiastic smile and an upbeat attitude.

Serving Refreshments

I call this serving refreshments, but it is essentially a polite gesture of welcoming people to your office with something small to drink.

Some offices serve cookies, but that's just something else to have to keep in stock and clean up after they're served.

This strategy only works if your company provides the supplies, but it is a very effective way of helping people adjust from the outside world to your model center and the presentation they are about to receive.

Just keep in mind that we aren't really serving anything nutritional — that's not the intent.

It's just a small beverage — coffee, hot chocolate, hot cider, lemonade, sweet tea, water, or soda, depending on your theme, budget, storage area, and time of year.

The concept is clear. This helps to put people at ease.

It gives them something to do while you're getting acquainted. It is a hospitable gesture that helps to offset any nervousness that people might have when they enter. In hot or cold weather, it's appreciated.

After you greet your customers with a smile, welcome them (with that specific word), introduce yourself, and learn who they are, you should offer them a refreshment.

Don't worry if you have to momentarily leave them unattended while you get the refreshments. This is so early in the process that they wouldn't think of walking out before you returned with something for them to drink because you haven't answered any questions or provided any information.

However, this is another great reason to keep your space in showroom condition because they will look around while you are out of the room.

Minding Your Manners

You, probably more than anyone else in your company, should be aware of and responsible for the physical condition of your new home sales or model center.

It is, after all, your space and your home base.

As I talked about extensively in the last chapter, make sure that clutter or poor housekeeping in your model center can't be used as a reason for someone to be unimpressed with the new homes that you are offering.

Don't let it be a factor for someone removing you from their short-list.

Many people will visit your sales center hoping to find reasons to eliminate your company from further consideration. Don't give them that chance when it comes to the way your model center looks.

Instead, give them every reason to be impressed with your attitude and the appearance of your sales center.

Remember to pick up empty beverage cups or containers and used napkins after each customer leaves your area. Inspect for and correct as necessary any spills from any beverages, "rings" on the furniture, or magazines left anyplace except where you want them.

If you have refreshments sitting out for your customers to access on their own, such as lemonade, cider, or coffee — or perhaps some cookies — make sure that they remain attractive, fresh, sanitary, appealing, and ready for the next customer.

There should be nothing out-of-place or anything unnecessary — paper, food wrappers, beverage containers (empty or not), leaves from indoor plants, mud, dirt, sand, rain, snow, or anything else that has been tracked in or blown in when the door was opened.

Vacuum, mop, dust, pick up, or otherwise remove what shouldn't be present.

If you are preparing mailing labels, typing letters, or doing other such activities at your work station, make sure you can stop what you are doing the instant someone enters your sales center — without making it look like you were doing something secretive that you didn't want anyone to see you doing — and that you can put all of your materials away quickly and neatly.

No one should be able to see information cards with the names of any other customers anywhere, and they should not be able to read mailing labels, outgoing correspondence, file folder labels, telephone messages, or anything else pertaining to the internal business of your company.

Be careful of what you are typing or what is displayed on your computer monitor also. Try to keep the screen from being visible to anyone but you. Wandering eyes can easily focus on a computer monitor screen.

Keeping the business of your company private is a responsibility that is often overlooked in the reception area.

Maintaining Your Focus

After taking all of the precautions to help people feel comfortable and impressed with what you are doing when they enter your sales or model center — your genuine smile, your enthusiastic attitude, the neat appearance of your reception area and displays, and the way you "welcome" them — this can be reversed quite easily by ignoring people or sending the signal that they are not that important after all.

How do you do that? By leaving them unattended for any period of time.

Therefore, don't lose focus and never let more than a couple of minutes pass without engaging them in some way if they are waiting for another team member to help them. Talk with them, get them another refreshment, or update them on how much longer it might be before the person that needs to help them is available.

Keep them involved and demonstrate that they are important and that you are interested in holding their attention.

Never leave your station while you have customers present. This includes making copies or even going to the restroom. The only exception is getting them a cup of coffee or glass of water. Otherwise, stay in your work area where you can see and talk with your customers and they can see and speak with you.

Imagine leaving your area to go do something else and finding that your customers have left while you were gone — even if it was just a couple of minutes.

You can't let them just walk out without having an opportunity to engage them.

If you absolutely must leave your area, have someone else cover for you and introduce them to your customers — explaining that you'll be right back.

7

Getting The Process Started

Learning Who People Are

After you have greeted and welcomed your customers to your community, it is time for you and your salespeople to learn who they are and what they are looking for so that your team can begin addressing their needs.

As I mentioned, you introduce yourself and then you get their names. Either they will respond to your introduction with their names, or you'll politely ask them for their names.

Then you must write them down on your information card. Even if you input those names into your computer, it's a good idea also to write the names down on a card or paper for two important reasons.

First you'll have it with you to refer to until you hand your customers off to a salesperson. Second, you can make pronunciation notes (and any other important information they share with you) directly on the paper or card so that you can make sure you are saying their names correctly — first names and last names.

Names are not always pronounced the way they look, and common sounding names (even first names that sound like "Katherine" or "Jonathan" or last names "Johnson" or "Myers") can be spelled various ways.

Never assume — always ask or confirm.

Get the name of every adult who is present that will be a part of the decision-making process — even if they don't seem very involved or talkative.

Using Your Card Effectively

As you are hearing people say their names, repeat them back aloud. Say it like you heard it.

If you said it correctly, they will nod or verbalize agreement. If you didn't get it quite right, they will assist you.

Keep saying it — along with their help — until you get it to sound the way they say it. Then use it immediately in your next question — for good measure.

Make whatever notes you need on your card for you to be able to say it correctly every time you address them by name.

Think of the advantage you'll have over people in other companies who didn't make the effort to learn their names, didn't take the time to make sure their names were being pronounced correctly, and didn't make the notes to be able to say it right a few minutes later.

People love being addressed by name, and they like hearing their name said correctly. Don't irritate or offend them by not attempting to use their name or by continually mispronouncing it.

The customer information card (and any computer record generated from it later) is your company's official record of each customer's visit.

You'll be passing it along to the sales representative who will be conducting the presentation, and he or she will add their notes to the card.

Both you and the salesperson will record a considerable amount of information on the card about your customers, such as their demographics, their needs, their experiences, what they have been shown, their interest level, their ability to make a decision on a new home, and any other information they share or that you observe.

Make any notes on the card that are appropriate for you to remember about your customers and their visits.

They are not going to be seeing the card or receiving a copy of it. It is strictly a tool for you and the sales representative to use as you help your customers look for and select a new home.

If anyone comments about your note-taking (and it would be rare for this to happen), just respond that you meet several people a day and that you want to keep the information straight.

Also, you don't want to forget anything important that they might have told you.

The Value of The Card

Ultimately it is the responsibility of the sales representative who works with each customer to get a completed information card about them. However, the process starts with you.

Since you are the one who initially greets each customer and begins to engage them in conversation, starting to fill in the customer information card is a natural part of your responsibilities.

The card is not something that you are being made to do just because it is required by someone in your company. It's much more valuable and important than that.

It is your company's official record of each customer visit along with all of the information on how to contact them again.

It also notes what they are looking for, what needs and requirements they have, and how you and your sales team have determined that you can help them.

Plan on getting the card started with each person or customer unit you greet, and the salesperson who works with them will add information and notes to it.

Eventually it will be the history of their home search with your company and the action plan for working with each customer.

It begins on their first visit on phone inquiry, and then you and your team maintain that customer record over time.

What Goes On The Card?

As you get the names of everyone who emails your office for information, calls on the phone, or walks through your front door, write them down on your card. Don't be concerned about their level of interest in what you are offering initially. Just get the names (and any other contact information you can obtain), and write them down.

Get the name of everyone present and anyone else who is mentioned as being part of the decision — as it is shared with you.

In addition to getting everyone's name, you want to record the mailing address of each customer unit, a good telephone number to reach them, and their email address (or more than one). You also need to record the correct date of the visit or the initial contact (if it precedes an actual visit).

These 5 items — date of the initial visit or contact, the names of everyone in the customer unit, the mailing address, a preferred telephone number for them, and a preferred email address — are considered essential information.

Anything else you can obtain about their needs or motivation is beneficial but not necessary before you have your customers meet with the person conducting the balance of the presentation.

A great way to record the date of the visit and to make sure that it is correct is to do it in advance.

As you start each day, take the number of cards that you think you might use that day (based on your history). If you're not sure, start with just a couple of cards. Then write the date on each card.

This way it will be correct, and it will be one less thing you will need to write down when you're talking with your customers.

If you need more cards later in the day, date some additional ones. If you find that you have dated too many and don't use all of them, you can use white-out, write over the date, or toss the extra blank card or two.

Keep in mind that you have the first opportunity to record this important information about each customer for your company.

Whatever you don't get done becomes the responsibility of the salesperson to complete, but try to get as much you can.

Challenge yourself to get complete cards for everyone.

Getting The Card Completed

In most sales centers that I have visited, the receptionists or the salespeople give the information card to their customers and ask them to complete it.

This is a very poor policy.

Why would you want your customers to do it? Don't they have enough on their minds when they enter your office?

This is your job responsibility. Do you really want to take a chance that your customers will supply incomplete or illegible information?

If your customers are filling out the form, what are you doing? Watching? Don't be a spectator.

Control this process. Take ownership of the registration.

Many receptionists (and salespeople as well) try to disguise or gloss over the fact that they need to make a record of the customer's visit, and they use such phrases as: *"Can you fill this out for me?"* *"I need you to fill this out,"* *"I need to have you complete this,"* *"My company makes us fill this out,"* *"Our marketing department needs this information,"* *"If it wouldn't be too much trouble, could you fill this out for me?"* or *"If you fill this out for me, I'll get you a brochure/a salesperson to talk to you."*

Obviously, your customers technically do not have to fill out the form or supply any information about themselves in order for a salesperson to talk to them.

They know that and you know that.

This creates an awkward situation that actually inhibits the sales process. Don't let it become a barrier.

It should just be a routine part of getting the visit started.

You have a good chance of getting compliance — especially when you request the information in a professional, gentle way — because people understand that you aren't trying to sell them anything or put any pressure on them.

Keep in mind that people just want information. They want a brochure and they want to see the models.

It just happens that they will need to meet with someone else on your sales team to get this information.

Now, what happens if someone refuses or declines to give you their address, email, or telephone number? Simply smile and say, *"That's okay"* or *"That's fine."*

It really isn't "fine," but then ask for another piece of information or get the salesperson to begin working with them (and let them get it from the reluctant customers later).

Avoid being confrontational. Keep it polite and professional.

The Total Customer Unit

When I speak about the "customer," I really mean the "customer unit."

This is the person, couple, family, or group — collectively — that will be making a decision on a new home.

When you meet and greet them in your sales center there often are members of the customer unit missing from the initial visit. If there are four people (or whatever the number) in the customer unit — even if not all are present — refer to them collectively as your customer rather than terming it four individual customers.

The customer unit may return at various times during their decision making process with more or fewer people than are present as you initially meet them.

However, collectively, the entire group of people that will be making the decision — from one person to a dozen or more — is what is referred to as the customer unit. For convenience, we often just call the entire customer unit, regardless of its size, "the customer."

An unaccompanied person might be present who is an unmarried single person, a person without their spouse or partner there, or a single parent without their children with them — regardless of how many people ultimately are part of the decision. Still, that single person could be the entire customer unit.

You might greet a male-female couple — either a married or unmarried couple with no children, none to occupy their new home on a regular basis, or with children not present with them at the initial meeting. Again, those two people could be the entire customer unit.

You might meet a husband-wife family with children present and additional children of various ages at home. Everyone in that family would be considered the customer unit.

It could be a husband-wife couple with no children to occupy their new home with them, and they would be the entire customer unit.

You might be working with another type of couple, such as two unmarried but related individuals (mother or father and an adult child, sisters, brothers, or cousins, for example) or two unrelated friends — regardless of apparent age differences or whether children are involved or not.

Then, there are the aunts, uncles, parents, grandparents, adult children and siblings, best friends, financial planners, attorneys, and others who won't be living in the home but may advise or impact the decision. They must be noted and factored into the decision-making process.

The point is that customer units come in various sizes and configurations, and you and your sales team won't know how large the customer unit is just by looking.

You'll need to ask questions.

The Fair Housing Act

Ultimately, you need to know who you're working with and how they might be related to each other — if at all.

You can introduce yourself to your customers and learn their names, but you can't assume anything about their relationships or family status — regardless of how it might appear to you.

You definitely can't come right out and ask either.

You need to have them volunteer this information for you, and then you can talk about it with them.

The Fair Housing Act doesn't permit questions about relationships, marital status, or family size.

As much as you might like to ask this, or as much as it appears people are related, you can't comment on it.

You can't ask anything that will appear to be discriminatory or suggest that anyone is or will be treated any differently than another.

While this is not your intention, it's still off limits.

You just want to get a better idea of who you are working with, but it could be construed that you will show homes to people or discuss your opportunities with them based on the way that they answer your questions.

That's why such questions are not allowed.

When There's Only One Person

Let's take a fairly common case that may be easy to misjudge.

When someone comes into your model home or sales center alone, it doesn't mean that they are single — and it doesn't mean that they aren't.

That's the point.

You can't tell about someone's marital or relationship status just by looking (whether they are wearing rings or not), and you can't come right out and ask them if they are married — or say anything about a spouse or partner.

You can ask if anyone else might be a party to the decision or if they'll need to consult with someone else before making a decision on a new home, but you can't establish or ask for the nature of that relationship until it is mentioned.

When they volunteer information about relationships or family members, you then can talk about it and discuss how other people that they mention might be involved in the buying decision.

If they say that they are single, fine.

However, you still need to know about other people who may be involved in the decision.

This could be children (either minor children at home or adult children living on their own), a fiancé/fiancée, parents, siblings, a friend, other relatives, a financial advisor, or an attorney — even if none of those people actually will be occupying the residence with your customer. They may not even return to look at the home with your customer.

On the other hand, if they say that they are looking for a new home along with their spouse, partner, fiancé/fiancée, friend, family, or children, then you may ask for the names of those other individuals and a little bit about their needs and interests. Of course, learn about the needs and interests of person in front of you.

Be sure to write down the information on your card —
along with the correct spelling. Put parentheses around
the names of the people who are a party to the
decision but not present to indicate that you need to
include them in the presentation but that you haven't
met them.

Just remember that you can't be the one to ask for this
information or to introduce it into the conversation.

You can just determine if they are making the decision
by themselves or if others will be involved.

Examples of such questions that you can ask include
"Are you looking for something for yourself?" or *"Will
this home be just for you?"*

You can also ask *"Will there be someone else (Is anyone
else) helping you make a decision (on your new
home)?"* or *"Is there anyone else involved in helping
you make a decision on your new home?"* or *"When you
find a new home that you like, will there be someone
that you'd like to show it to and get their opinion?"*

When Two People Are Together

When two men, two women, or a man and a woman
enter your model center *together*, they might appear
to have some type of relationship — but you cannot
assume anything.

Relationships aren't always as they seem.

You need to clarify who is actually looking for the new home or participating in the decision.

They might be related in some way, and they might not.

One of them might just be "tagging along" with the other — while that other person is house-hunting.

Just as you would with a person who is alone, you need to ask a clarifying question about others that might be assisting or advising them in the decision.

This doesn't assume or imply that they will need help or that they are incapable of making a decision without the input and participation of others.

It's simply for clarification and confirmation — especially since you don't know anything about relationships until they are revealed.

Similar to the questions you might ask an unaccompanied person, you can ask them if anyone else (not present) will be assisting them or participating in their decision on a new home, or if they plan on coming back with anyone to show them what's available and get their input or opinion before they make their final decision on a new home for themselves.

Family Size Can't Be Assumed

Even if two people appear to be husband and wife or introduce themselves to you in that way, you can't make any assumptions about family size or anyone else who might be participating in the decision.

Regardless of their age, they might be relying on the opinions, advice, or contributions of children (at home or grown and living on their own), parents (living with them or living on their own, local or out-of-the-area), friends, relatives, or other advisors.

If two men (or two women) come into your model center together, one of them might be looking for a new home with their friend (who is just there to accompany the other one), or they could be looking for a home to occupy together — whether they are related or not.

Each could be looking separately for a new home — to occupy alone or with others — and just decided to visit your model center together.

If they happen to be related in some way, such as brothers, sisters, cousins, parent and adult child, grandparent and grandchild, nephew and uncle, niece and aunt, brothers-in-law, or sisters-in-law, they still might not intend to occupy the new home together — and you won't be able to tell just by looking at them.

You must ask questions to determine who is looking for the new home and who might be there for support — or if there are others not present who will be involved in the decision at a later time.

Nothing Can Be Assumed

The point is you just don't know how — or if — people are related to each other, how they will occupy a new home, how many people will be living in the new home, or who might be making or influencing the decision.

You can't assume anything. Always keep this in mind.

You must ask questions.

You need to learn who is interested in the new home, who is making the decision, who might be an influencing or consulting party to the decision, and who will be occupying the new home.

You must find out who in your customer unit is making or influencing the purchasing decision so that you and your sales team can focus on making your presentation to include the appropriate person or individuals.

This is true whether any or all of these other influential people are present at your initial meeting. In fact, you or your sales representative might not ever meet or speak with them.

Getting Past The Basics

After collecting the essential contact information of name, address, phone number, and email address, you can move on to learning a little more about your customers and what prompted their visit.

Then, note any responses that you get on your customer card.

Your customers might actually make this fairly easy for you.

As you are greeting them, they may volunteer why they have visited you or how they heard about you.

For instance, as soon as they walk in, they may request to see your models or ask if you have models for them to see. They might say that they have an appointment or ask to see a particular salesperson. They might mention that they saw an ad in the newspaper, that they saw a directional sign, that they visited your website, or that a friend of theirs recommended that they come by to see what you have to offer.

They could also volunteer what they are looking for in a new home in terms of builder's reputation, size, layout, floorplan, location, amenities, or price range and that this is what prompted their visit to your community.

They might even mention that they just came from looking at a competitor (or even more than one) — that they mention by name of the builder or the community — and that they want to see how you compare.

Just remember the importance of the contact information. This is vital to have.

If they walked out the door as soon as you captured the information (hopefully this doesn't happen), at least someone in your company would have a way to contact them again and continue the discussion about your homes.

Also, be careful to avoid using the word "salesperson" in conversation, as in "*Have you talked with one of our salespeople yet?*" or "*I'll get a salesperson to help you.*"

People do not want to talk to a "salesperson." They do not want to be "sold." They just want information. Tell them that you will get someone to "help" them.

It's OK if they mention it, just don't verbalize it yourself.

Reason For The Visit

If they do not volunteer or suggest the specific motivating factor for their visit, then you need to ask them if they have been to your community or spoken to anyone previously about your homes (either in-person or by telephone).

Learning if people have had any previous contact with your community is more than a formality. It may tell you something about their motivation for visiting this time, and it can help you determine what they might already know about what you are offering.

If you or someone else already started a customer record about them, you can locate it and begin adding to it instead of creating another one.

If this is their initial visit, then you and the sales staff know that they will require a complete presentation on this visit — time permitting — to become acquainted with your company, your location, and the opportunities available in your homes or community. Keep in mind the short-list.

After asking your customers if this is their initial contact with your community, you then want to ask them how they learned about your community — if they have not volunteered this information already.

Both of these questions — the one about previous contact with your community and the one concerning how they learned about your community — sound like nice, friendly questions. They are. That is why they are used as a part of the greeting and welcoming process.

However, they have a much more important purpose so be sure to incorporate them into your conversation with each customer.

Learning More About The Source

There are two appropriate ways to ask someone how they learned about your community.

Be careful not to ask someone what brought them in. While this might sound just like a semantical difference or synonym for how they heard about or learned about you, it can lead to a silly response such as their car, their spouse, or something to that effect.

One approach for learning about the attraction source is to ask, "*How did you happen to hear about* [insert the name of your community]*?*" or "*How did you happen to hear about our community/us?*"

You want them to tell you what they recall using without any prompting from you. You can ask if they used various sources, but you are interested in what they remember on their own.

In response to your question, people could recall seeing an ad in the paper, having visited your website (directly or through a search engine), having had a friend tell them about your homes or your location, knowing someone who lives in your community or owns one of your homes, having had a Realtor® tell them about it but not accompany them, or coming in with a Realtor®.

They also might mention seeing a sign or billboard, hearing about it on the radio (even if you don't advertise there), reading an advertisement in a magazine, or literally being unaware of your community until seeing it from the road.

Unless you are located on a well-traveled roadway or are easily visible from one, be wary of the "drive by" response. Usually some other motivating factor is the reason for the visit, such as noticing one of your ads, visiting your website, or looking for a home in this particular area or neighborhood.

"Driving by" tends to be a catch-all category of non-specific responses about the reason that people are visiting your community. Many people use this response because it usually isn't challenged or questioned — even when driving by isn't such a logical answer.

If people actually had no prior knowledge of your community and literally were just driving by and saw your location for the first time, then this could be an appropriate response — one that would suggest (subject to confirmation) that they are looking for something in your immediate area or that this area is important to them.

The second way of asking how someone learned about your community or your new homes is to ask if they saw an ad in your local newspaper or if they have visited your website.

If either, or both, is the case, find out what appealed to them or caught their attention, make a note of it, and discuss that with them.

Also, learn if people used more than one source to learn about you, such as seeing an ad and then visiting your website. Ask what appealed to them in each of the sources.

Asking people how they learned about your community might sound like a marketing question, but it actually can help reveal what is important to them in their search for a new home.

It also gets them to open up and start talking about their needs and interests.

8

Being A Valuable Team Member

Doing Your Part

Most people — particularly if they are really interested in looking for a new home — will oblige you with their name, address, email, and telephone number when you request it. You aren't asking them for anything different than any other builder they might visit.

The main thing that might be different from other builders is that you are doing the asking and then writing the information down for them instead of giving them the card and making them do all of the work.

You can't force people to cooperate and honor your request to furnish their contact information, but such a refusal essentially labels them as someone who won't be doing business with your company anyway.

For anyone seriously looking for a new home — regardless of when they are ready to purchase — they will have no problem sharing their contact information with you.

You'd like to get 100% cooperation, but don't worry about the few people who won't comply with your request. The sales representative will have an opportunity to get it later.

If both of you are unsuccessful in getting this important information, this customer is not someone worth pursuing for a sale.

Some people will need to feel more comfortable with your company and will wait until they have established somewhat of a friendship or professional relationship with the salesperson to be able to share their contact information with them later in the presentation. That's OK as long as someone in your company gets it.

Nevertheless, you will have welcomed everyone to your model or information center and started the process of collecting the customer information.

The Transition

Unless you are busy greeting or working with other customers that have entered your sales center and this prevents you from personally introducing your customers and your salesperson to each other, you should make it a point to transition your customers from your care to the salesperson who will be helping them.

You know everyone's name — and how to say them all correctly — so each can hear all the other names pronounced properly.

Give the customer information card to the salesperson and point out anything that you want to call to his or her attention.

Graciously thank your customers for visiting and return to your station. Wait for your next customer unit to arrive.

If your customers are finished with the refreshments you gave them, collect their cups or glasses and dispose of them. Ask if they need something else to drink, and take care of that as they begin working with your salesperson.

If none of your salespeople are available, or if there is to be a delay, explain to your customers that it will be a few minutes before anyone is available to help them.

Just remember that when someone enters your sales center they should never feel that they have been left unattended, abandoned, or ignored — or that they are unimportant.

Remember as well that people don't want to wait to talk to a "salesperson" but just to someone who can help them.

They may know that they need to talk to a salesperson, but they don't need to be reminded that you want to "sell" to them.

Your company has invested a significant sum of money in advertising and marketing to attract people to visit your community, and providing that you have something that meets their needs and budget, you want people to like you well enough to seriously consider living in one of your homes and to return for another visit — possibly a decision-making one.

Unless you make it onto someone's short-list by impressing them that you can meet their needs as well as or better than other builders they are considering, you will not have any chance of earning their business and making a sale.

Multi-Tasking

When you are busy greeting or talking with your customers, be aware of other people who may enter your sales center and walk right past you to proceed directly to the site plan or displays, mingle with other customers, or attempt to approach a salesperson directly.

Take the initiative and walk over to them.

Welcome them to your community, shake hands with them, and learn who they are.

Don't wait for them to approach you, and don't leave them unattended or unacknowledged.

You can lead them back to your reception desk or counter to complete an information card with them, or you can carry an extra card with you to fill out as you meet them where they are standing. You might even be able to sit with them briefly to do this.

If you are not certain if you should speak to someone in your sales center, err on the side of talking with them.

It is better to ask them if they are being helped than to have them feel ignored or left wondering why someone has not engaged them yet.

The Hit-And-Run Customer

From time-to-time, some customers will rush into your sales center "to take a quick look" at your models or get a brochure (trying to avoid talking with a salesperson).

I call these people "hit-and-run" because they just want a brochure and that's about it — few (if any) real questions are asked and no engagement is desired with anyone on the sales team.

People think they can avoid meeting with a salesperson by breezing in and getting a brochure from you.

They may even request that they be shown the way to your models and allowed to look by themselves because they are in a hurry or just want to get some "decorating ideas" or "see what you've done."

Sometimes people leave their engine running or the car door open — or leave their kids or spouse in the car — while they run it to get your brochure.

Unfortunately, this tactic won't work for them because you don't — and shouldn't — have any brochures available.

It's not your place to be handing out brochures.

People don't need a brochure before they've even learned what you offer or determined that they might be interested in what you offer. That comes after they talk with a salesperson.

You likely have something on your website that they could look at or download anyway, but asking for a brochure just seems to be a necessary part of looking at new homes.

When you don't have your brochures made up in advance and sitting on the counter — or on a table or credenza in public display — it is very easy (as well as honest) for you to tell people that you don't have the brochures available.

Simply tell them that you would be happy to have someone answer their questions (or speak to them for a moment) and get them a brochure.

This takes all of the responsibility for the delivery of the brochure away from you and ensures that, at a minimum, someone on your sales staff has at least spoken with that customer.

Some people may decide that it's just too much effort to get your brochure and leave without sharing any information. Don't take it personally.

More On Conveying The Brochure

In order for someone to get a brochure, they will need to speak to a salesperson. It's that simple.

Keep in mind that a brochure is nothing more than reference material.

The customer is not "owed" a brochure — especially without you (and your sales team) knowing more about their needs.

It is not your responsibility to hand out brochures.

It is a sales function — regardless of how other sales centers and builders regard this. They may choose to give out brochures to anyone who requests one or to have them sitting out for the taking. That doesn't mean that your company has to do it this way, too.

There must be a face-to-face connection — however limited it might be — between the customer and the sales representative.

If someone is unhappy with that, let them leave without the brochure. They quite likely were not serious about what you are offering anyway.

Think of it as the "agree" button that you have to click on updates, apps, or programs before they will install on your computer or smartphone. You may not agree with every provision, but what choice do you have if you want their software installed?

You click "agree" because you want the program or the update. Likewise, your customers will comply if they want the brochure.

It is highly unlikely that anyone would actually make such an important decision as buying their new home by just having and looking at a brochure. Nevertheless, some people act as if this is how it is done.

Much or all of the information in your brochure may be on your website anyway, but you shouldn't be the one who gives out brochures.

Also, they shouldn't be generic. They should be personalized to address what the customer is looking for or reflect what has been discussed or shown to them.

Your salespeople are the only ones who can determine what to include in each customer's brochure — and only after they have met with each customer and discussed their needs.

The Brochure Exception

The only exception to this rule of you not handing out brochures to people who request them is for you to be able to get one for someone who already lives in your community or someone who is in the process of having their home built by your company — for them to give to a friend or co-worker.

A Realtor® who has been to your model center previously might come in and ask you for another copy of your brochure to show to someone they are working with or intend to bring to your community.

In such cases, it's okay for you to get them a basic brochure from a salesperson.

You really don't have any brochures available in your work area and will need to go directly to your sales staff or their offices to get one.

It will necessarily be a general brochure because there is no way to personalize it with just information that pertains to their home search since they aren't the one looking for the new home.

However, try to learn (and record) the names of the people for whom the brochure might be given.

Only give out one brochure at time though.

If a homeowner or Realtor® asks you for multiple copies of your brochure — for whatever reason — refer them to a salesperson to field their request.

Engaging Realtors® When They Enter

When Realtors® visit your sales center — with a customer or when they come in alone — welcome them to your community (like you do with everyone else who visits unless you know that they have visited previously and then you can say "*welcome back*").

Learn their name, and fill out an information card for them or for their customer — whichever applies — unless you know they have been there before and have returned without a customer.

If they are alone conducting a preview visit, enter their information on a customer information card. Just note on the card that it is a Realtor® preview visit so that everyone is aware of the nature of the visit.

If they are returning — for whatever reason such as an appointment or to ask a specific salesperson questions — just note the return visit and the nature of it on their information card or computer record so you have a history of that visit.

If they have a customer with them complete a broker participation agreement in addition to the customer information card for the customer unit that they have brought.

Fill out the broker participation agreement yourself as you would your customer information card — do not hand it to the Realtor® for completion.

This way you can read your writing when you're done, you can make sure that you have all of the required information without needing to review the form and ask for additional information (as you might need to if you have them fill out the form), and you can help to guard against having them supply their own contact information when you really need that of the customer.

Also, this does not disengage them from their customer the way it would if they had to fill out the card.

There might be a short wait before they can speak with a salesperson. If so, treat them as you would any other customer — regardless of whether they are alone or have brought a customer with them.

Offer them a refreshment (and their customer, of course) and keep them informed as to when someone will be available to help them.

Sometimes when a Realtor® comes into your sales center with a customer, they may try to act as a filter for the customer by answering questions for them.

If this happens, direct your questions directly to their customers — even if the Realtor® persists on answering for them.

Try not to accept *"Mr. and Mrs."* in lieu of the customer's first names, and do not accept the office or cell phone number of the Realtor® as the contact number for the customers.

Attempt to learn their first names, and strive for the actual contact information for the customers.

The Realtor® can instruct the salesperson on how they might want to be contacted after the visit, but you need the customer's phone number for their customer record. It may be the only opportunity to gain this important piece of information.

Noting Telephone Callers

I've already talked about greeting people on the phone when they call for information.

You also want to make a record of their call and start a customer information card about them — for your salesperson to use to get back in touch with them or to use when they arrive for a presentation.

People who telephone for information should not get the impression that they are interrupting anything, even if they are.

You should answer each telephone call as if that is your only function and that you were awaiting their call.

Of course, not all calls will be initial contacts to your community or even calls directly about sales.

Certainly many calls will be from people wanting information on what you are offering or asking for directions.

However, some calls will be from customers who have already been working with your salespeople who are calling them to ask a question, to confirm or reschedule an appointment, or for a related matter.

Some calls may be from purchasers or homeowners.

They could be calling with warranty concerns, with the names of friends of theirs who would like to see your homes, or just to ask a question.

Some incoming calls might be from lenders, appraisers, construction personnel or other people who are working with your company. They would be calling to speak to someone else in your company, and you would be the one answering the incoming calls before directing them to the person requested.

Some calls could be internal in the sense that they are from others in your company to someone else in your company — or perhaps for you with some information you requested.

Some calls may be solicitation calls from vendors wanting to do business with your company.

Some could even be wrong numbers.

When a person is contacting your company for the first time with sales questions, obtain their name (and note the correct pronunciation) and a call-back telephone number before turning them over to a salesperson.

As a receptionist, you actually may have an easy time of getting people to give you a call-back phone number, but there are a few good ways to do this: just come right out and ask people for their telephone number, tell them that someone else will need to call them back to help them, or tell them that you are helping someone else and will need to call them back in a few minutes.

You also could mention that sometimes people get cut off when you attempt to transfer them to someone who can help them (a salesperson).

All of these reasons for needing their phone number seem plausible.

If you have caller ID, you can ask them if the number they are calling from that is displaying on your phone is the number where they can be reached.

In such cases where you have caller ID service available, never assume that the number they are calling from is a good call-back number.

They could be calling from a business establishment where they happened to be, from their place of business through a switchboard, from a neighbor or relative's home, or from a location they will be leaving momentarily.

Always ask for a good call-back number or confirm that the number displayed is a good one for them. Be sure to write that number down immediately before another call comes in and replaces the number on your display.

Obviously, you cannot be successful in getting a telephone number from someone you have never met who really does not want to give it to you, but you should be successful more times than not in getting a call-back number for them.

You Are An Important Team Member

Finally, never think of yourself or verbalize that you are "*just a receptionist.*"

The word "just" should not be an adjective to describe yourself or anyone else in your company.

No one is *just* a receptionist, or *just* a hostess, or *just* a secretary, or *just* a security guard, or just any other position in your company.

Everyone is part of the team and has an important role to play.

Everyone in your company has a valuable function to perform, and everyone helps your company to be successful.

Everyone in your company has a sales function of some sort, and is quite important for that role.

Your position is particularly valuable because you are the one who primarily greets the public for your company and helps to create a positive initial impression.

As we have discussed, in most cases, you are the first person to come in contact with your company's customers — whether by email, telephone, or in-person.

Your company's valuable customers represent both a substantial investment in attracting them and potential revenue in the form of a completed transaction.

Ultimately, they represent a referral base and additional sales revenue.

Therefore, as you prepare to greet or speak to each customer that enters your sales center, telephones for information, or contacts your office by email from your website, remember that there are two very important people involved.

One of the important people, of course, is the customer. The other is you and the valuable contribution you make.

Now, It's Up To You

The concepts, tips, recommendations, and strategies that I present in this book are for you to use in greeting the public, welcoming them to your sales center, creating an outstanding first impression, adding professionalism to your position, and keeping your company on their short-list until your sales team can make a sale.

Now, it's up to you to take as many of these concepts as you can and begin incorporating them into your daily routine.

If you need someone to consult as you putting these concepts and strategies into effect, contact me. I'll be happy to discuss them with you.

Have fun greeting and getting to know your customers as you represent you company with an unparalleled professionalism.

Steve Hoffacker

Steve Hoffacker, AICP, CAASH, CAPS, CGA, CGP, CMP, CSP, MCSP, MIRM, is principal of Hoffacker Associates LLC, a new home sales training and real estate coaching company based in West Palm Beach, Florida.

Steve is an award-winning new home sales trainer and coach, commercial real estate broker, marketing consultant, award-winning photographer, best-selling author, blogger, teacher, and salesman.

For more than 30 years, he has helped homebuilders, new home salespeople, Realtors®, small business owners, and other professional salespeople to be more visible, competitive, profitable, and effective — and to really enjoy themselves as they pursue their business.

Steve understands the importance of the customer experience and your role in helping to shape and create that when people contact you or visit your model center.

He wants you and your company to be successful and has created this guide to help make that happen.

This book will be a great resource for you to help you understand your customers and how to work with them effectively.

Use these strategies and concepts for your professional success.